MW01129621

This Easter book is presented to

Emelia Ann Persell

by

Grandma Mary Persell Martin

on

Easter Sunday April 16, 2017

The Easter Story

Drawn directly from the Bible

Edward A. Engelbrecht
Gail E. Pawlitz
Editors

CONCORDIA PUBLISHING HOUSE • SAINT LOUIS

1 2 3 4 5 6 7 8 9 10   18 17 16 15 14 13 12 11

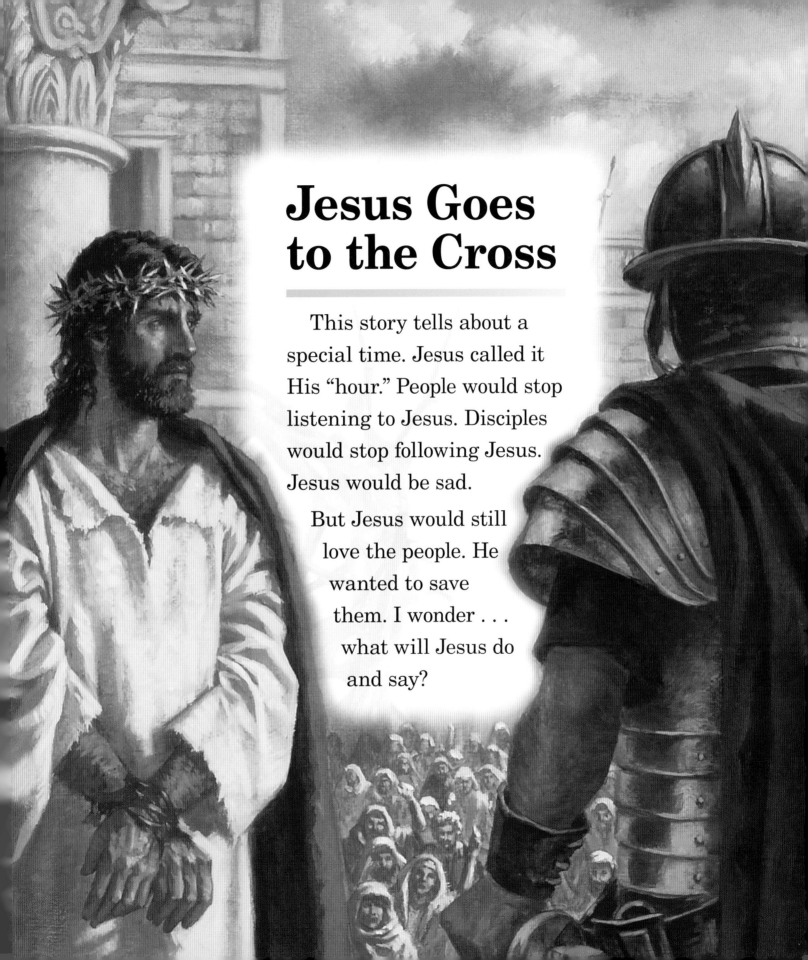

Jesus Goes to the Cross

This story tells about a special time. Jesus called it His "hour." People would stop listening to Jesus. Disciples would stop following Jesus. Jesus would be sad.

But Jesus would still love the people. He wanted to save them. I wonder . . . what will Jesus do and say?

The Triumphal Entry

humble

mounted

cloaks

Hosanna

stirred up

Matthew 21

The crowd drew near to Jerusalem. They came to the Mount of Olives. Then Jesus sent two disciples. He said to them, "Go into the village in front of you. You will find a donkey tied, and a colt with her.

Untie them and bring them to Me." This took place to fulfill what was spoken by the prophet:

"Behold, your king is coming to you.

He is humble and mounted on a donkey."

The disciples went and did as Jesus said. They brought the donkey and the colt. They put their cloaks on the donkeys, and Jesus sat on them.

Ask

What animal did Jesus ride into Jerusalem?

What did the crowd do when Jesus came by?

How did the people praise God?

Do

Wave streamers or scarves and say, "Hosanna" or "Lord, save us."

Pray

Dear Jesus, You are my Savior who has come triumphantly to save me. I will sing to You and praise You too. Amen.

Most of the crowd spread their cloaks on the road. Others cut branches from the trees and spread them on the road. And the crowds were shouting, "Hosanna to the Son of David! Blessed is He who comes in the name of the Lord! Hosanna in the highest!"

When Jesus entered Jerusalem, the whole city was stirred up. People said, "Who is this?"

And the crowds said, "This is the prophet Jesus. He is from Nazareth of Galilee."

Jesus entered the temple. He drove out all who sold and bought in the temple. But the blind and the lame came to Jesus. And He healed them.

The chief priests and the scribes saw the wonderful things that Jesus did. They saw the children crying out in the temple, "Hosanna to the Son of David!" The leaders became mad. They said to Jesus, "Do You hear what these children are saying?"

Jesus said to them, "Yes; have you never read in the Psalms,

" 'Out of the mouth of infants and nursing babies God has prepared praise'?"

The Lord's Supper

Luke 21–22

Every day, Jesus was teaching in the temple. But at night He stayed on the mount called Olivet. Then early in the morning all the people came to Jesus in the temple to hear Him.

Now the feast drew near. It is called the Passover.

The chief priests and the scribes were seeking how to put Jesus to death. Judas went to the chief priests and officers. Judas told them he would betray Jesus to them. And they were glad. They agreed to give Judas money.

Then came the day on which the Passover lamb had to be sacrificed. So Jesus sent Peter and John, saying, "Go and prepare the Passover for us. Then we may eat it."

Then the hour of the feast came. Jesus reclined at table. The apostles were with Him. He said to them, "I have desired to eat this Passover with you before I suffer. For I tell you I will not eat it until it is fulfilled in the kingdom of God."

Passover

betray

reclined at table

remembrance

covenant

Jesus took bread. When He had given thanks, He broke it. He gave it to them. And He said, "This is My body, which is given for you. Do this in remembrance of Me."

And likewise He took the cup after they had eaten. He said, "This cup is poured out for you. It is the new covenant in My blood. But behold, the hand of him who betrays Me is with Me on the table."

And the disciples began to question one another. They wondered which of them it could be. ✠

Ask

Look at the story picture. What are Jesus and His disciples doing?

What is Jesus saying?

Who will eat the bread and drink the wine?

Do

Ask a parent to help you make unleavened bread. Unleavened bread is similar to the bread Jesus gave His friends and to the bread we use in Holy Communion.

Pray

Dear Jesus, help me to remember always that You died on the cross for me. Amen.

passion

bound

governor

crucified

innocent

The Passion of Christ

Matthew 27

When morning came, all the chief priests and the elders of the people made plans against Jesus. They wanted to put Him to death. So they bound Him. They led Jesus away to Pilate the governor.

Now Jesus stood before the governor. The governor asked Him, "Are You the King of the Jews?"

Jesus said, "You have said so." But He gave him no other answer. So the governor was greatly amazed.

At the feast the governor often released a prisoner whom the crowd wanted. The governor had a prisoner called Barabbas. He had killed people. So when the crowd gathered, Pilate said, "Whom do you want me to release for you: Barabbas, or Jesus?"

They said, "Barabbas."

Pilate said to them, "Then what shall I do with Jesus?"

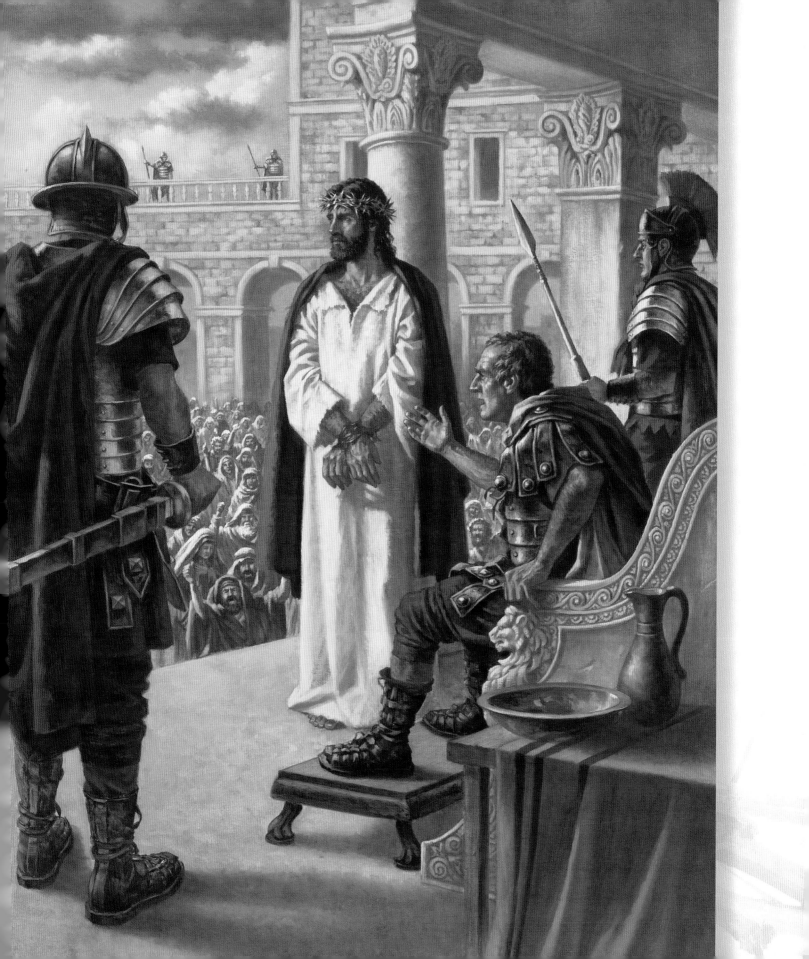

Ask

What did the people want Pilate to do to Jesus?

For whom did Jesus die on the cross?

Do

Count the crosses in your home.

Each time you find one, say, "Jesus died for me."

Pray

Dear Jesus, I am sad when I see pictures that show how people were mean to You. Thank You, Jesus, for suffering and dying on the cross to take away my sins and give me a home in heaven. Amen.

They all said, "Let Him be crucified!"

And he said, "Why, what evil has He done?"

But they shouted all the more, "Let Him be crucified!"

So Pilate took water and washed his hands before the crowd. He said, "I am innocent of this man's blood. See to it yourselves."

And all the people answered, "His blood be on us and on our children!"

Then Pilate released Barabbas.

The soldiers of the governor took Jesus. They stripped Him. They put a red robe on Him. They twisted a crown of thorns. They put it on His head and put a reed in His right hand. And kneeling before Him, they mocked Him. They said, "Hail, King of the Jews!" And they spit on Him and struck Him on the head.

Then the soldiers led Jesus away to crucify Him. ✠

Jesus Dies and Lives Again

criminals

dazzling

apparel

Luke 23–24

The soldiers led Jesus away. They seized Simon of Cyrene and laid the cross on him. He carried it behind Jesus.

Two criminals were led away to be put to death with Jesus. They came to the place that is called The Skull. There they crucified Jesus and the criminals. One was on His right, and one was on His left.

And Jesus said, "Father, forgive them. For they do not know what they do."

The people stood by, watching. But the rulers and the soldiers mocked Jesus.

One of the criminals said to Jesus, "Are You not the Christ? Save Yourself and us!"

But the other said, "Do you not fear God? This man has done nothing wrong."

12

Ask

Where are
the women in the
story picture?

What are the
angels saying
to the women?

Where is Jesus?

Do

Blow Easter
bubbles.

What's inside the
bubble? Pop one
and find out.

The bubbles are
empty. The tomb
was empty too.

Pray

Dear Jesus,
You can do
anything! You
even can come
back to life!
Thank You
for dying to pay
for my sins.
Thank You
for making it
possible for me
to live forever in
heaven with You.
Amen.

And he said, "Jesus, remember me when You come into Your kingdom."

And Jesus said, "Truly, I say to you, today you will be with Me in Paradise."

There was darkness over the whole land. Then Jesus called out with a loud voice. He said, "Father, into Your hands I commit My spirit!" And He breathed His last.

Now there was a man named Joseph. He took down Jesus' body. He wrapped it. And he laid Jesus in a tomb cut in stone. The women who had come with Jesus from Galilee followed. They saw the tomb.

On the first day of the week, the women went to the tomb. They found the stone rolled away from the tomb. But when they went in they did not find the body of the Lord Jesus.

Then, behold, two men stood by them in dazzling apparel. The men said to the women, "Why do you seek the living among the dead? Jesus is not here. He has risen!"

Jesus Rises from the Grave

Jesus suffered under Pilate. Jesus was crucified, died, and was buried. But on the third day He rose again from the dead!

The disciples were afraid. They did not want Jesus to die. They did not understand that He would rise again. I wonder . . . how will Jesus teach them? How will they see that Jesus is alive?

16

The Resurrection of Jesus

John 20

Early on the first day of the week Mary Magdalene came to the tomb. It was still dark. She saw that the stone had been taken away from the tomb.

So she ran back to Peter and another disciple. She said, "They have taken the Lord. We do not know where they have laid Him."

So Peter ran with the other disciple to the tomb. The other disciple reached the tomb first. He stooped to look in and saw the linen cloths.

Then Peter went into the tomb. He saw the linen cloths. The face cloth was folded up by itself.

Then the other disciple also went in. He saw and believed. Then the disciples went home.

linen cloths

Rabboni

My brothers

Ask

Who went to the tomb early on Easter morning?

What was Mary Magdalene's surprise on Easter?

Do

Make play dough Easter eggs and hide them.

Ask your family to hunt for the eggs. When all the eggs are found, tell your family about Mary's Easter surprise.

Pray

Dear Jesus, I am so glad You are alive. Help me tell others this good news. Amen.

But Mary stood crying outside the tomb. As she wept she stooped to look into the tomb. There she saw two angels in white. One angel was at the head and one at the feet of where Jesus' body had been laid.

They said, "Woman, why are you weeping?"

She said, "They have taken my Lord. I do not know where they have laid Him." Then she turned and saw Jesus. But she did not recognize Him.

Jesus said, "Woman, why are you weeping? Whom are you seeking?"

Mary thought the man was the gardener. She said, "Sir, if You have carried Jesus away, tell me where He is."

Jesus said, "Mary."

Then she said, "Rabboni!" (which means Teacher).

Jesus said, "Do not hold on to Me. Instead, go to My brothers. Say that I am going to My Father and your Father. I am going to My God and your God."

Mary Magdalene went and told the disciples, "I have seen the Lord." ✝

Jesus Appears on the Emmaus Road

Luke 24

On the day Jesus rose from the dead, two men were going to a village named Emmaus. It was about seven miles from Jerusalem. As they walked, they talked about Jesus' death and the empty tomb.

While they were talking, Jesus came near. He walked on with them. But the two men did not know it was Jesus.

Jesus said, "What are you talking about?"

They stood still. They looked sad. Then Cleopas said, "Don't You know what things have happened these days?"

He said to them, "What things?"

They said, "Things about Jesus. Our priests and rulers put Him on a cross to die.

"He did many wonderful things. We had hoped that He was the one to redeem Israel. It is the third day since He died. And some women amazed us. They were at the tomb early this morning. When they did not find His body, they came back. They said they had seen a vision of angels. The angels said Jesus was alive.

village

tomb

redeem

vision

vanished

19

"Some people with us went to the tomb. They did not see Jesus there."

Jesus said to them, "But Jesus had to suffer." And He explained the Scriptures about Himself.

When they came near the village, Jesus acted as if He were going farther. But the two men said, "Stay with us. For it is evening. The day is almost over."

So Jesus stayed with them. When He was at the table, He took the bread and blessed it. Then He broke it and gave it to them. At once, they were able to recognize Him. But He vanished from their sight.

They said to one another, "He helped us understand the Scriptures." Then, they got up and returned to Jerusalem. They found the eleven disciples, who said, "The Lord has risen indeed! He has appeared to Simon!" Then the men told what had happened on the road. They told the disciples how they saw it was Jesus when He broke the bread. ✝

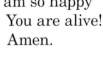

Ask

What happened while the two men were walking to Emmaus?

What did Jesus do for them?

What happened after Jesus vanished?

Do

Choose a partner. Take a walk and retell the Bible story.

Pray

Dear Jesus, thank You for giving me Your Word so I can hear about what You did for me. I am so happy You are alive! Amen.

Jesus Appears to Thomas

appears

Holy Spirit

signs

John 20

On Easter evening, the disciples locked the doors. They were afraid of the Jews.

Jesus came and stood among them. He said, "Peace be with you." Then He showed them His hands and His side.

The disciples were glad. Jesus said to them again, "Peace be with you. As the Father has sent Me, I am sending you."

Then He breathed on them and said, "I give you the Holy Spirit. If you forgive the sins of anyone, they are forgiven. If you do not forgive their sins, they are not forgiven."

Thomas was not with them when Jesus came. So the other disciples told him, "We have seen the Lord."

But Thomas said, "Unless I see in His hands the nail marks, and place my finger in them, and place my hand into His side, I will never believe."

Eight days later, Jesus' disciples were inside again. This time Thomas was with them. The doors were locked, but Jesus stood there. He said, "Peace be with you."

Ask

What does Thomas say to his friends before he sees Jesus?

What does Thomas say to Jesus after he sees Jesus?

Do

Look carefully at the picture of Thomas and Jesus.

Can you find the nail prints on Jesus' hands?

Can you find the scar on Jesus' side?

Pray

Dear Jesus, thank You for loving Thomas so much and helping him to believe that You were alive. Help me believe in You forever and ever. Amen.

Then He said to Thomas, "Put your finger here, and see My hands. Put your hand in My side. Believe."

Thomas said, "My Lord and my God!"

Jesus said, "Do you believe because you see Me? Blessed are those who have not seen Me and yet believe."

Jesus did many other signs with His disciples. Not all of them are written in this book. But these are written so that you may believe that Jesus is the Son of God. And by believing you may have life in His name. ✝

24

Jesus Ascends into Heaven

John 21; Acts 1

When Jesus was arrested, all the disciples ran away. Peter denied Jesus three times. But now things would be different.

Jesus said to Peter, "Do you love Me?"

He said, "Yes, Lord. You know that I love You."

Jesus said, "Feed My lambs."

A second time Jesus said, "Peter, do you love Me?"

Peter said, "Yes, Lord. You know that I love You."

Jesus said, "Tend My sheep." A third time Jesus said, "Peter, do you love Me?"

Peter was very sad that Jesus had asked him the third time. Peter said, "Lord, You know everything. You know that I love You."

Jesus said, "Feed My sheep." Later, Jesus said to Peter, "Follow Me."

Peter turned. He saw another disciple whom Jesus loved. He was following them. Peter said, "Lord, what about this man?"

tend

Mount of Olives

witnesses

gazing

Ask

What question did Jesus ask Peter three times?

How did Jesus show His love?

Where did Jesus go?

Will Jesus come back?

Do

Cut a cloud out of paper.

Write these words on the cloud: [Jesus said,] "I am with you always" (Matthew 28:20).

Play hide-and-seek with the cloud. Remember that even though Jesus has gone to heaven, He promises to be with us always.

Pray

Dear Jesus, thank You for going to prepare a wonderful home for me in heaven. Help me to listen to Your Word while I wait for You to come again. Amen.

Jesus said to Peter, "What is that to you? You follow Me!"

Jesus showed the disciples that He was alive for forty days. He spoke to them about the kingdom of God.

Jesus also told the disciples to stay in Jerusalem. They were to wait there for the promise of the Father. Jesus said, "You will be baptized with the Holy Spirit in a few days."

Later, Jesus led them to the Mount of Olives. They asked, "Now will You bring back the kingdom to Israel?"

He said, "You do not need to know what God does. But you will get power when the Holy Spirit comes to you. You will speak God's Word in Jerusalem. You will be My witnesses to the end of the earth."

As the disciples were looking, Jesus was lifted up. Then a cloud took Him out of sight.

The disciples were gazing into heaven as Jesus went up. And behold! Two men stood by them in white robes.

The men said, "Men of Galilee, why are you looking into heaven? Jesus will come back the same way as you saw Him go into heaven." ✝

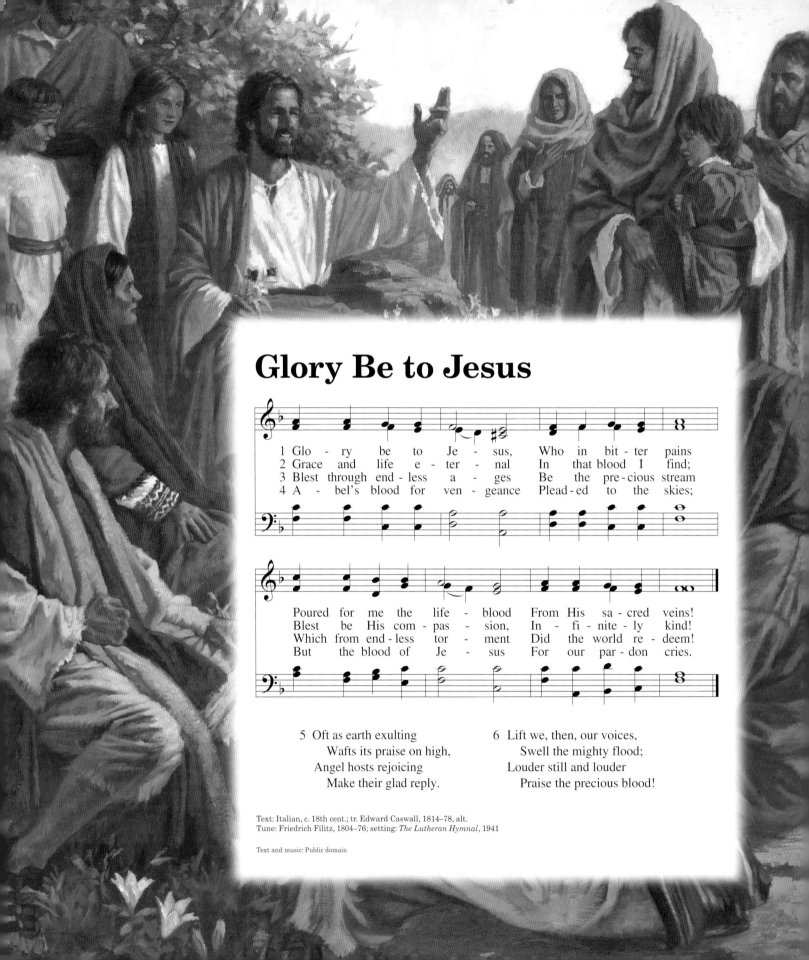

Glory Be to Jesus

1 Glo - ry be to Je - sus, Who in bit - ter pains
2 Grace and life e - ter - nal In that blood I find;
3 Blest through end - less a - ges Be the pre - cious stream
4 A - bel's blood for ven - geance Plead - ed to the skies;

Poured for me the life - blood From His sa - cred veins!
Blest be His com - pas - sion, In - fi - nite - ly kind!
Which from end - less tor - ment Did the world re - deem!
But the blood of Je - sus For our par - don cries.

5 Oft as earth exulting
    Wafts its praise on high,
    Angel hosts rejoicing
    Make their glad reply.

6 Lift we, then, our voices,
    Swell the mighty flood;
    Louder still and louder
    Praise the precious blood!

Text: Italian, c. 18th cent.; tr. Edward Caswall, 1814–78, alt.
Tune: Friedrich Filitz, 1804–76; setting: *The Lutheran Hymnal*, 1941

Text and music: Public domain